ILLUSTRATION GUIDE

FOR ARCHITECTS, DESIGNERS AND STUDENTS

8-16,

CONTENTS

INTRODUCTION

In my career as a professional illustrator, I discovered that most successful commercial artists make extensive use of a filing system known as a "scrap file". This assemblage of information is sorted and filed using a method unique to artists.

It seemed only reasonable that a "scrap file" could also have its uses in the field of architectural illustration. Although techniques and styles differ considerably in this profession, several elements are universally used in almost all renderings. Trees, people, plants, and vehicles add interest and scale to all building drawings. An illustrator must have the ability to place these items within a drawing so as to enhance the overall composition and complement the building.

A professional delineator is expected to possess the talents needed to create a finished rendering. But what about the architect, designer or student who must create a rendering without the help of a professional delineator? The architectural design process requires studies in three dimensions at several preliminary stages. Often, the client's first view of his project is in the form of a designer's perspective study. The client's reaction to this first presentation can virtually make or break a design concept.

The second step in the rendering process is usually the presentation to a planning board or financial institution. Again, the reaction to the perspective view can spell success or failure for the project. It only stands to reason then, that an architectural illustration should be created with the best tools available, and this book, with its hundreds of illustrations created especially to complement architectural and industrial design presentations, is just such a tool.

The sections containing people, trees, plants and vehicles have been indexed to make selection of the proper item quick and easy. If you will take the time to read the section on how to use this book, you will find several shortcuts that may save you many hours of rendering time. This book is designed to be an important drafting room tool, and so, just like a pencil or T square, you must learn to use it properly.

The *Illustration Guide* was created to make available to the architect, designer and student the same material used by professional illustrators.

HOW TO USE THIS BOOK

The secret formula for creating good renderings is very simple: build a strong perspective drawing. There exist today several acceptable methods for the formulation of a perspective:

1. The two elevation system
2. The top plan system
3. The measuring point system
4. The cube system

Each has its champions, so it's up to you to decide just which method suits your purpose. After 20 years of professional renderings, I have found that the "cube" method best serves my need for quick, accurate layouts.

Building the Perspective

1. Selection of view

Most renderings are structured from plans and elevations. These drawings are usually in scale, so horizontal and vertical measurements are marked on the drawing.

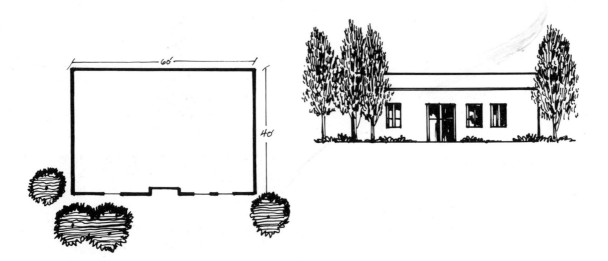

Using a 30° – 60° triangle, select your proposed station point on the plan.

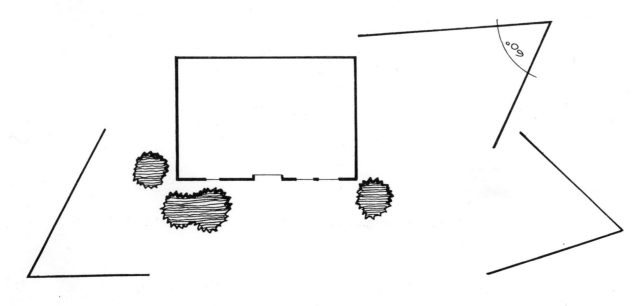

Make quick freehand studies of each proposed view.

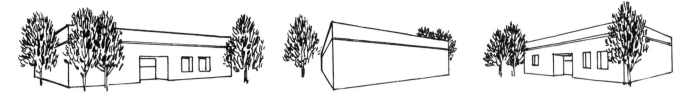

At this stage in the development of your perspective, you must choose your eye level and the distance you wish to be from the building (station point).

2. The full size block-out

At this point you are satisfied with the view and the eye level has been established. Projecting the quick study up to finished drawing size requires a few momentous decisions:

A. Selection of the size of the finished drawing (let's try 24″ x 36″)

B. Selection of the size of the building within the borders

C. Creation of a pleasing composition

It should be noted here that the sample building we are using is quite simple and that your project is probably more complicated. The fact is, the "cube" method makes the degree of complication irrelevant. Whatever you need to draw, be it our simple box building or the Eiffel Tower, can be easily constructed using this perspective method.

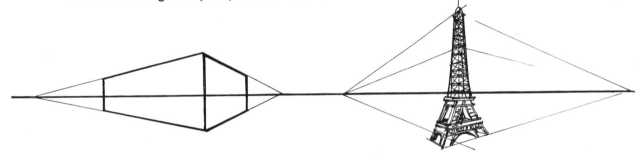

If you feel more confident with the plan projection method of perspective, just remember, as you're setting up your projection system, the rest of us have already begun to draw details in *our* building.

Anyhow . . .

The use of this book as a guide does not require the selection of any particular perspective method, just an *understanding* of whatever method you choose.

• THUMBNAIL SKETCH

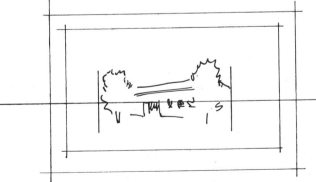

Using your "thumbnail" sketch as a guide, plan the picture composition on the full size sheet.

Selection of Vanishing Points and a Vertical Scale

Your quick thumbnail sketch has in fact established the station point (the spot the viewer of this particular perspective has chosen, i.e., the position of the eye). In the sample drawing, the station point is located on the plan as shown.

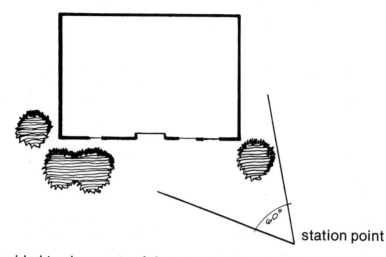

station point

We have decided to view more of the south elevation than the east so our left-hand vanishing point (vp) will be somewhere off the paper.

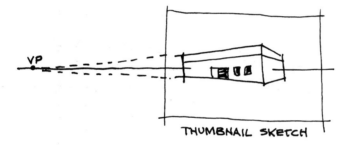

VP

THUMBNAIL SKETCH

But, you say, "How can I locate my vanishing point so far off the paper? My drawing board is only just slightly larger than my paper". Using a T square, build a simple arc system to locate that elusive off-the-board vanishing point.

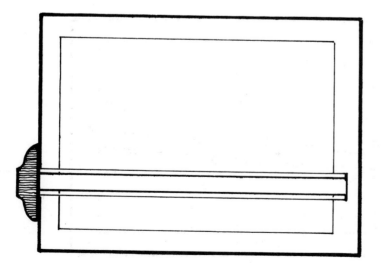

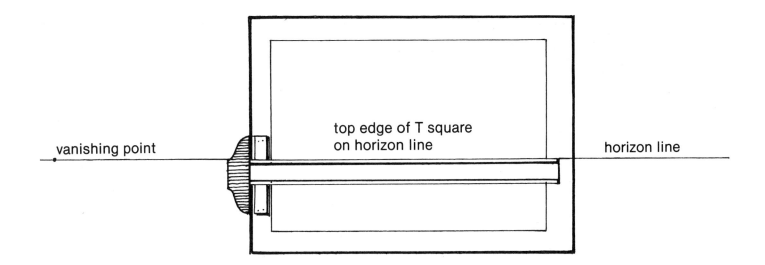

vanishing point   top edge of T square
on horizon line   horizon line

Attach a section of heavy mat board *exactly* the length of the head of your T square to the drawing board (but off the surface of the paper). This piece of mat board is the first section of an arc that will locate the left vanishing point.

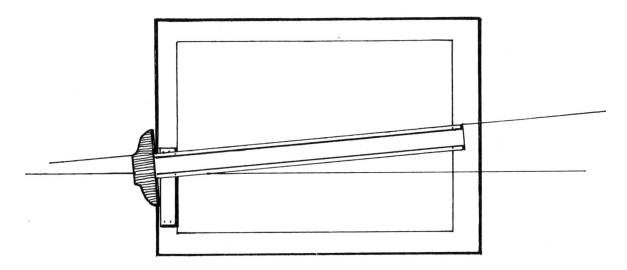

Resting your T square on the mat board strip, draw an angle that closely duplicates the perspective angle you selected on your thumbnail sketch.

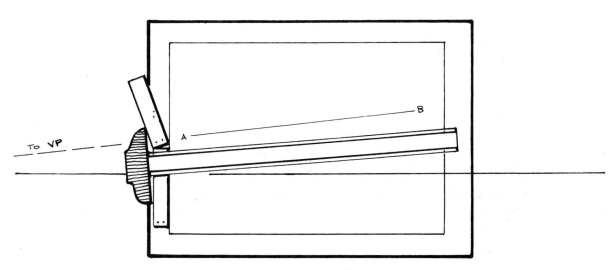

11

Connect Point *A* to Point *B* and secure a piece of mat board exactly the size of the first section to your drawing board. This arc will give you all of your vanishing lines *above* the horizon. Duplicate the procedure for the bottom vanishing lines and you have found your impossible left vanishing point.

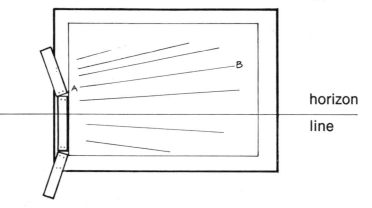

The Vertical Measuring Line

Let's review what we have done so far:

A. We have selected a viewing angle and eye level (the thumbnail sketch).
B. We have located the horizon line on the full size paper and found the left-hand vanishing point.
C. We have estimated the size the building should be in relation to the rest of the picture.

Now we must locate the vertical measuring line and the right-hand vanishing point.

We know from the thumbnail sketch that we wish to see more of the south face of the building. This means that the leading edge of the building will be somewhere to the right of center on our drawing.

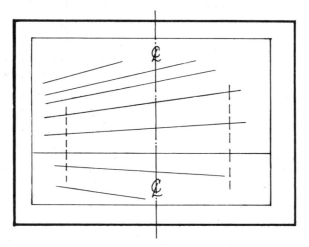

It also means that the right-hand vanishing point will be closer to the center than the left vanishing point.

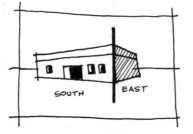

Choose the percentage of south and east faces (back to the thumbnail) and draw the nearest vertical edge of the building on your paper. This vertical is usually used as the vertical measuring line.

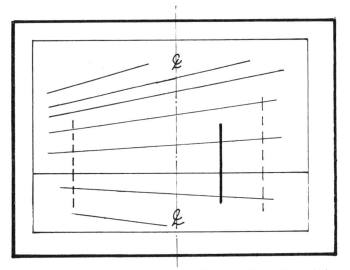

We know from the plans that the building is 22' tall and that the south face is 60' long. By measuring the distance from the vertical height line to the left-hand limits of the building area we can develop a scale that will allow the building to fit within our prescribed borders.

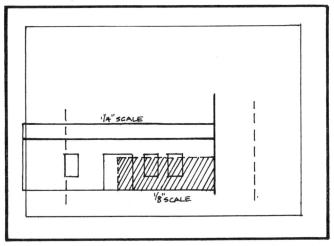

We know that the perspective will diminish the horizontal measurement, so it is just possible that the ¼" scale might fit our need. Let's try it. First select an eye level at 5'6" and plot that on the vertical. This gives us the base of the building and a way to locate figures within the picture.

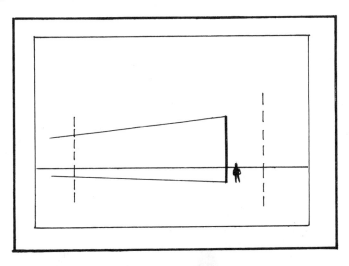

Now let's select the right-hand vanishing point. We know it must fall outside the right-hand edge of the building, and for the sake of sanity, lie within the confines of the drawing board. (One constructed arc per drawing should be enough for anyone.) Let's place it 3" from the right edge of the building limit.

By connecting the top and bottom points to the right-hand vanishing point, we have established our building in perspective.

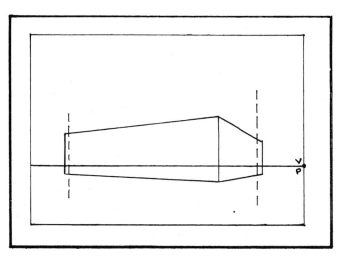

Creating the Measuring Cube within the Perspective

Using the ¼" = 1' scale we have chosen, mark off 22' on the vertical height line beginning 5'6" (in scale) below the horizon line.

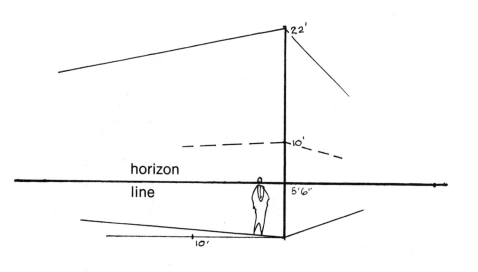

Measure 10' on the vertical height line and 10' on a line parallel to the horizon line beginning at the base of the vertical height line. We know that measurements diminish in perspective, so the line indicating the base of the building will be shorter than the horizontal measuring line. This measurement is subjective at best, but when you create the measuring cube within the perspective and it *looks* like a cube, then for all intents and purposes, your perspective measuring system will be close enough.

14

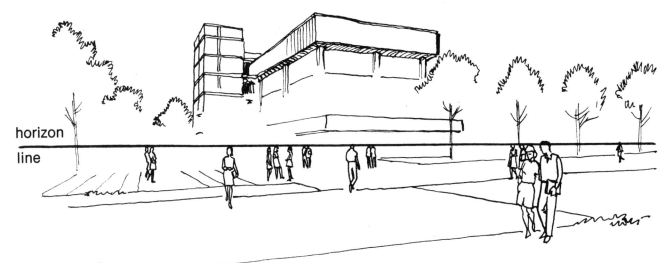

horizon
line

horizon line

17

RENDERING HINTS

RENDERING HINTS

VIEWING ANGLES

The viewing angle on this rendering was taken at about five
and a half feet *above* the plaza. When using the Illustration
Guide figures in a rendering with the horizon line this far
above the people, you must make adjustments in the drawing of the figures to conform to the perspective (Fig. 1 & 2).

Figure 1   Figure 2   21

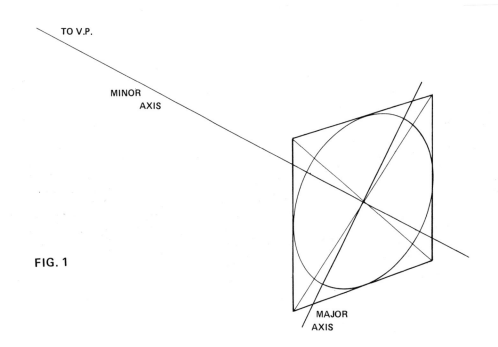

FIG. 1

CIRCLES & ELLIPSES

With the advent of modern technology, circular buildings are easier to build but are still just as hard to draw as ever. These pages illustrate three important facts about circles in perspective.

Figure 1 shows the circle in perspective (ellipse) in a square also in perspective. The minor axis bisects the center of the ellipse and connects with the left vanishing point. It is called the minor axis because it crosses the ellipse at its narrowest dimension. The major axis connects the farthest dimension of the ellipse.

Figure 2 applies the illustration in Figure 1 to architectural drawing. Notice how the ellipse recedes in degrees as it recedes in perspective.

The two renderings illustrate that the major axis is always parallel to the horizon line when viewed from above or below.

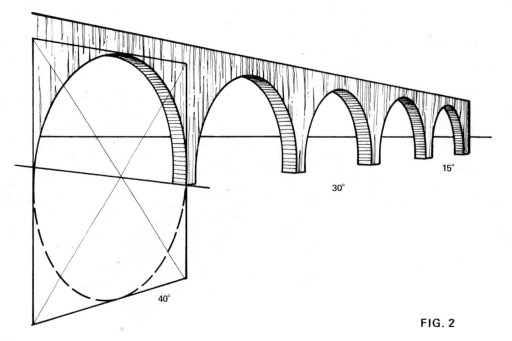

FIG. 2

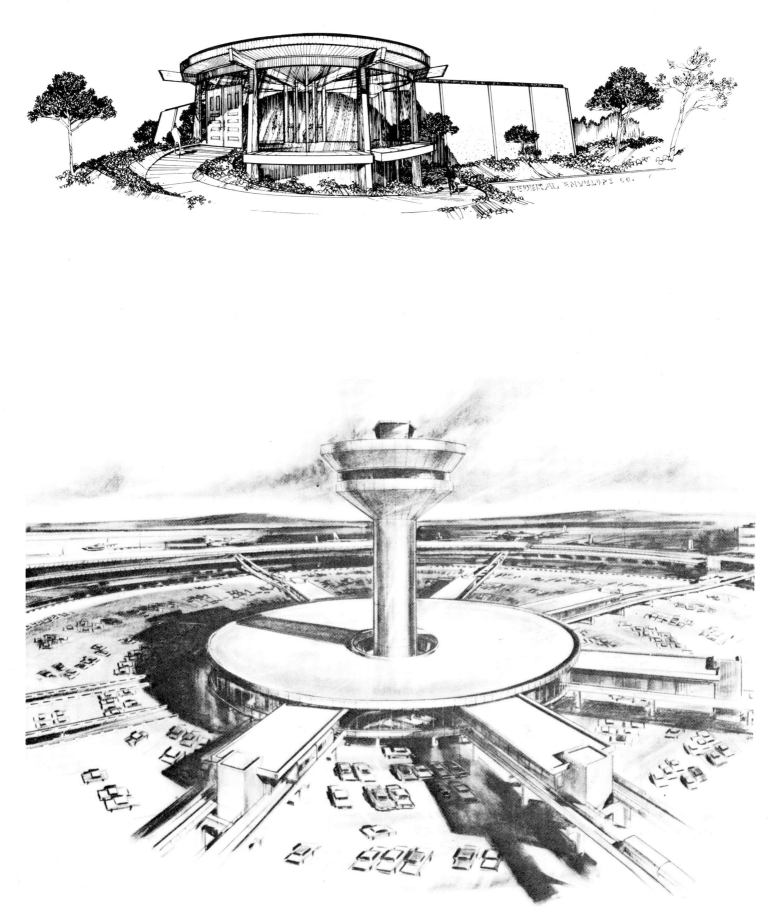

INTERIORS

The two renderings on these pages are both "one point" perspectives. However, Figure 1 has the vanishing point slightly off to the right. Normally, the placing of the vanishing point in this fashion would force a second vanishing point to the far left on the horizon line, but interior sketches seem to work better if we just ignore that rule and draw just as if the vanishing point were in the center of the picture.

HORIZON LINE

Figure 1

HORIZON LINE

Figure 2 has a different problem. The podium is several steps below the main floor. Each row of chairs must be constructed to be slightly below the row behind. Naturally, the figures must be below the horizon line at the podium, but remember, only *one* horizon line may be used.

Figure 2

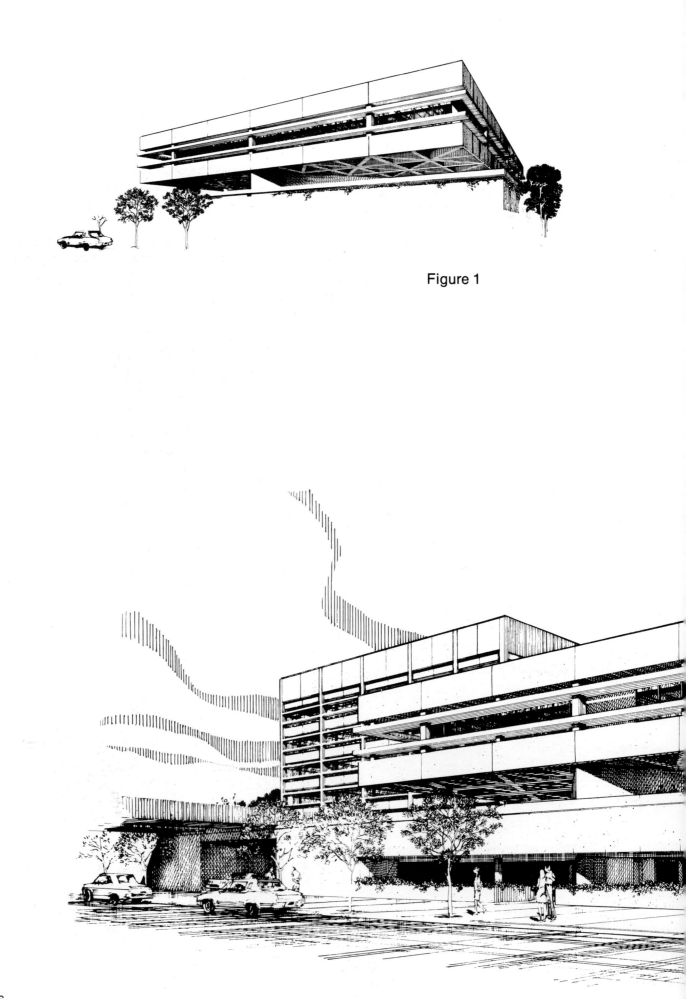

Figure 1

PEN AND INK

When you have to make changes (note several between Figures 1 and 2), take care not to damage the paper when you erase. If the paper shreds, make a patch using identical paper with transparent tape on the *back* of the paper.

If you don't wish to make direct copies (black line, sepia, etc.), you can use white paint for minor changes. Be sure to do your ink work first, as the pen won't function well over white paint.

Figure 2

VIGNETTES

This composition illustrates a central entry area within a large government complex. A one point perspective was chosen to best show the actual feeling a person would have when approaching the entry area. Notice how you "almost" see through the glass.

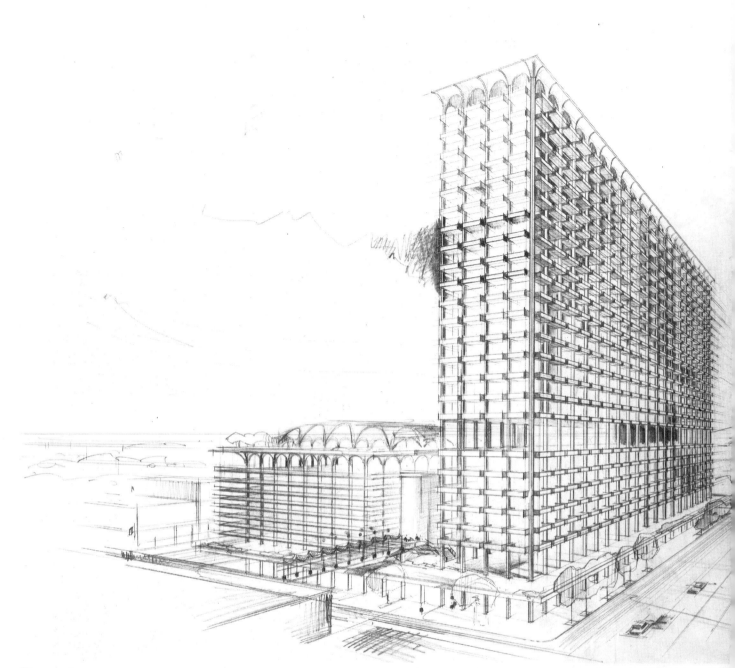

Figure 1

AERIAL VIEWS

Figure 1 is a rough pencil sketch made in preparation to painting a finished watercolor(Fig.2).The eye level was established at about the eighth floor to help show the relationship between the building and the street area. The final drawing was transferred to a watercolor board *after* most of the problem areas had been solved in the preliminary sketch.

Figure 2

The viewing angle in Figure 3 is much higher than Figure 2 because the relationship between the building elements and the surrounding area was critical. The rendering was done with airbrush over an ink drawing. The final ink sketch was photographed *before* the airbrushing to give the architect the maximum reproduction options.

Figure 3

Figure 1

Figure 2

GLASS

The three illustrations on these pages indicate the basic approach to glass indication. Figure 1 is a watercolor sketch showing a standard double-hung window with drapes. The shadow area on the glass is lighter than the sun-lit area and the darker areas of glass give just a hint of the room beyond. Glass is a lot more reflective in shadow, so use your own judgment. Remember, the final result is what counts. Figures 2 and 3 indicate a "sketchy" approach to rendering that can often create a mood that is lost in more finished renderings.

Figure 3

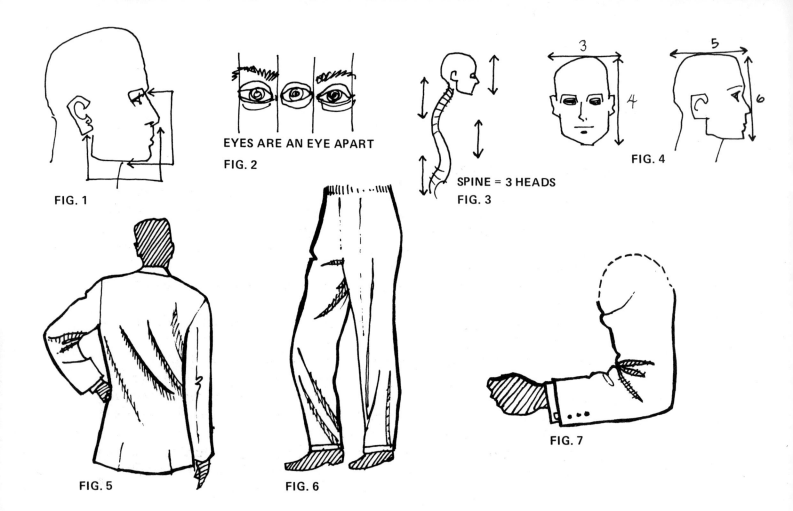

EYES ARE AN EYE APART
FIG. 2

SPINE = 3 HEADS
FIG. 3

FIG. 4

FIG. 1

FIG. 5

FIG. 6

FIG. 7

When drawing the figure, even if you stylize or just block in shapes for scale, proportion and attitude are important features to draw properly if your rendering is to achieve success. The viewer identifies with the people in your drawing and it is not all that difficult to draw people properly.

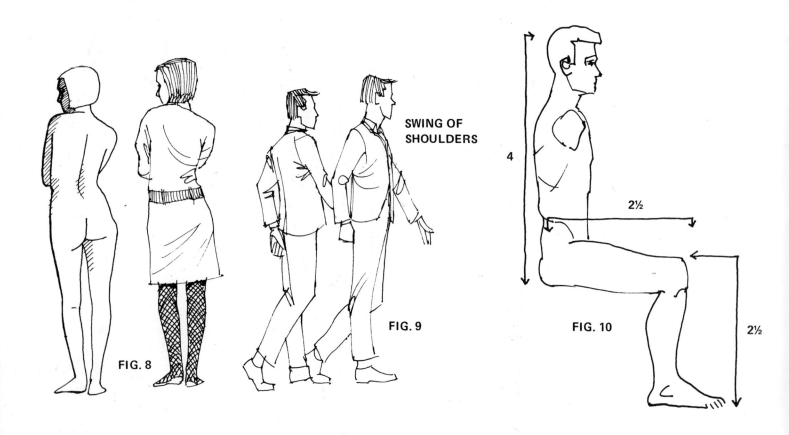

SWING OF SHOULDERS

FIG. 8

FIG. 9

FIG. 10

4

2½

2½

DRAWING PEOPLE

These pages contain several illustrations showing basic proportions and attitudes. As figures are an important aspect of architectural rendering, the knowledge of proper proportions is equally important.

Figure 1 illustrates that the distance from the eyes to the chin is roughly equal to the distance from the ear to the tip of the nose.

Figure 2 shows spacing between the eyes, and Figure 3 shows that the spine is three heads tall.

Figure 4 draws your attention to the proportion of both front and side views of the head.

Figures 5, 6, & 7 illustrate folds most commonly found in men's suits.

Figure 8 shows a girl standing with her weight on one leg. Notice how the hip on the side that bears the weight pushes upward and out. The leg carrying the weight of the body bends in so that the foot positions itself directly under the head.

Figure 9 shows that when walking, the body turns from side to side, thrusting the shoulders foreward on the opposite side of the body carrying the weight.

Figure 10 illustrates basic proportions of the seated figure.

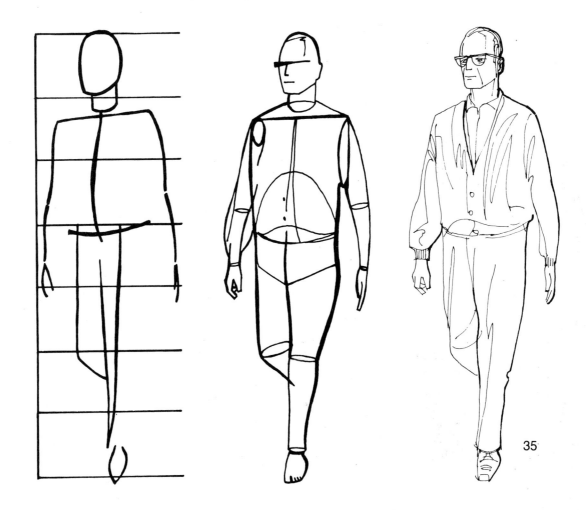

35

Figure 1

WATERCOLOR RENDERING

One of the most useful tools in the preparation of architectural renderings is the medium of watercolor. Available in tubes from Winsor Newton or Grumbacher and applied with a soft sable brush, watercolor rendering is fast and offers a wide range of textures and colors.

A minimum range of colors is suggested for architectural work. A typical palette is shown in Figure 3.

Figure 1 shows the degree of completion the pencil drawing should be in before the application of color. Remember, watercolor is a transparent medium so lines will show through. Make sure you have the shadows roughed in and the direction of sunlight secured before you proceed with the painting.

Figure 2

Figure 2 illustrates the first wash to apply to the rendering. First tape the edges of the building with Magic Mending or drafting tape. Don't use masking tape as it will pull the paper surface. I use a watercolor board with the paper already mounted on it. If you don't use a board you must make a "stretch" or your paper will buckle and large washes will be impossible to accomplish. Use a handmade 300 lb. paper and you won't have to worry about buckling.

To apply a large wash, such as the sky, wet the entire area (except for the areas you want to leave white) with a large sable brush. Mix the desired color in a cup and "drop in" the color without touching the paper with the brush. Pour the excess off by tilting the board. Be sure to pour off the top and don't get any on the building.

Figure 3

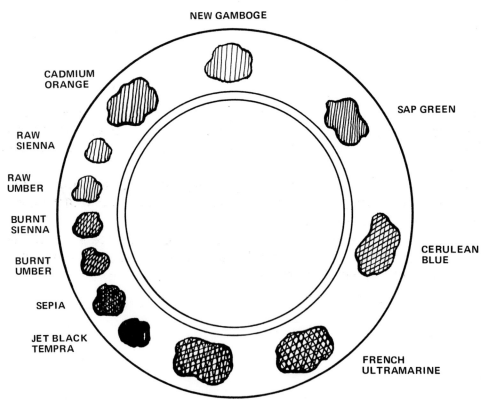

NEW GAMBOGE

CADMIUM
ORANGE

SAP GREEN

RAW
SIENNA

RAW
UMBER

BURNT
SIENNA

CERULEAN
BLUE

BURNT
UMBER

SEPIA

JET BLACK
TEMPRA

FRENCH
ULTRAMARINE

PRUSSIAN BLUE

Figure 4

After the sky dries, begin to render the building (Figure 3). Notice gradations from dark to light in the shadow areas. Try to accomplish the desired tone in one wash. The less over painting you have to do the faster and cleaner your painting will be.

Figure 4 is the finished rendering. Details are completed and rough edges are cleaned up with opaque white. You can mix your watercolors with opaque white to touch up little problem areas.

On the first few renderings you do, it is helpful to prepare a "rough" before actually attempting the final painting. Plan your shadows and composition carefully before doing the finished work.

COMPOSITION

Architectural illustration requires a plethora of talents from knowledge of instrumental perspective to practical application of artistic drawing techniques. To prepare a really good illustration, one of the first things you must know is the proper approach to good composition. Art students spend many hours arranging blocks and cones and spheres, studying old master paintings, and generally struggling with elements within a picture to gain even a rudimentary knowledge of composition.

Figure 1

Figures 1 & 2 show a simple building and the most common elements of architectural rendering: sky, people, trees, cars, plants and paving. Both drawings contain all these elements and both are the same building. Four simple steps of proper composition make Figure 1 more successful than Figure 2. Figure 1 selects a 3/4 view from 4' high vantage point. The front of the building is displayed prominently. Figure 2, on the other hand makes no attempt to display the front of the building and the view selected takes no advantage of the foreground. Several elements complicate Figure 2. The tree in the foreground splits the picture in half, the sidewalk becomes a confusing shape and the building shadow does not help define the entry but instead becomes a strange shape on its own accord. Foreground people should look into the picture or at least participate in activities conducive to what is going on in the picture.

Figure 2

SUNLIGHT & SHADOW

Figure 3 illustrates a shadow cast by sunlight on a cube. Notice that lines A and B are parallel. You do not create a "vanishing point" for sunlight as the sun is too large and far away to be affected by pictorial perspective.

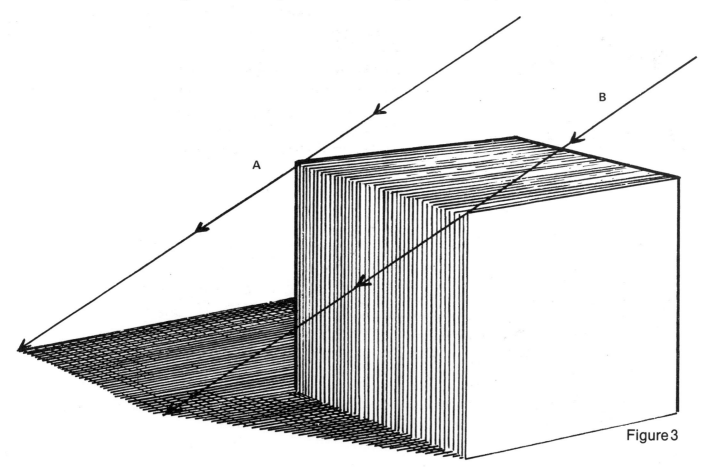
Figure 3

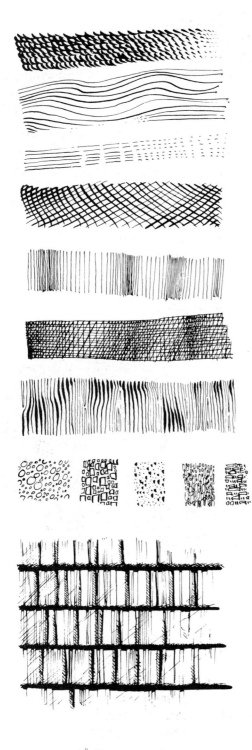
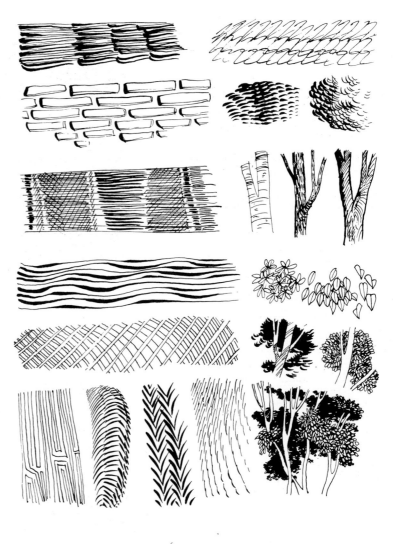

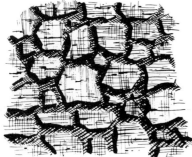

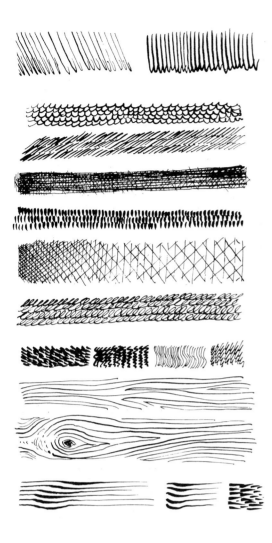

TEXTURE

One of the most important aspects of architectural illustration is the treatment of texture. These pages illustrate shingles, brick, rock and a variety of different pen strokes. Copy the textures on these pages or make up your own. Don't be afraid to experiment.

PEOPLE

SCALE 1/8" = 1'

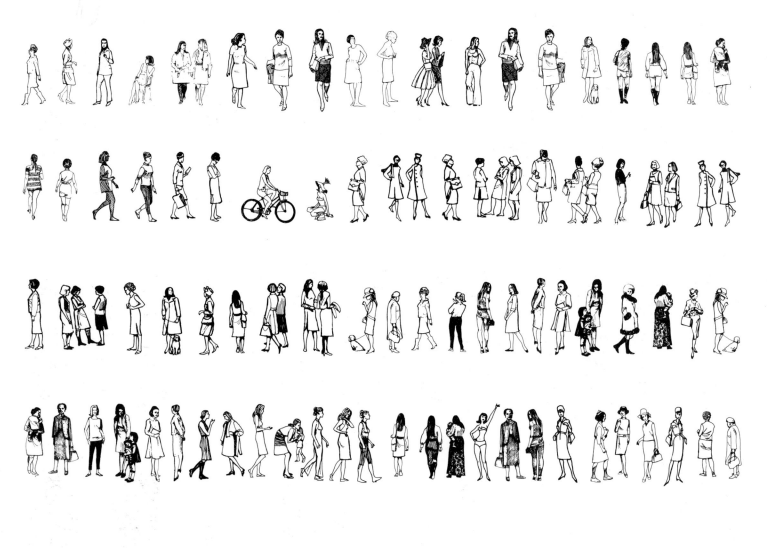

SCALE 1/4" = 1'

SCALE 1/4" = 1'

SCALE 3/8" = 1'

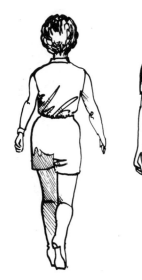

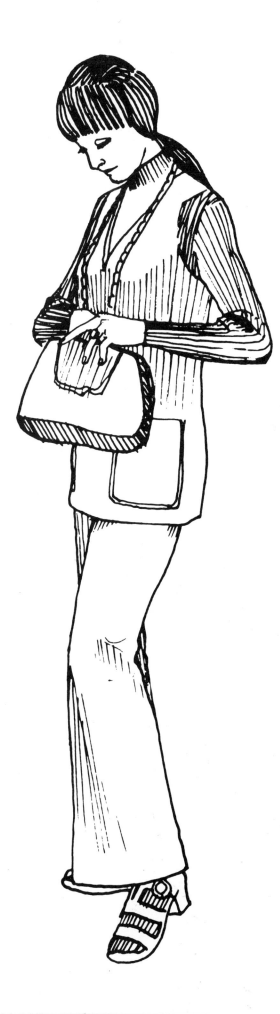

PEOPLE

SCALE 1/8" = 1'

SCALE 1/4" = 1'

SCALE 1/2" = 1'

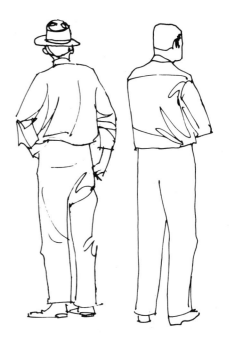

SCALE 1/2" = 1'

SCALE 1/2" = 1'

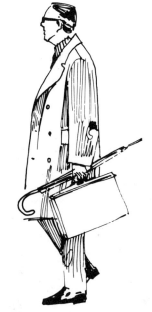

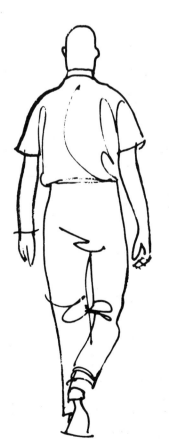

PEOPLE

GROUPS

SCALE 1/8" = 1'

SCALE 1/4" = 1'

SCALE 3/8" = 1'

SCALE 1/2" = 1'

SCALE 1/2" = 1'

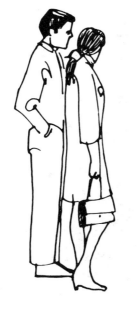

SCALE 1/2" = 1'

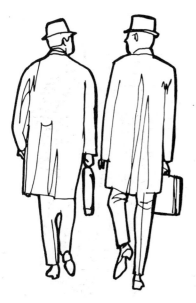

SCALE 1/2" = 1'

SCALE 1/2" = 1'

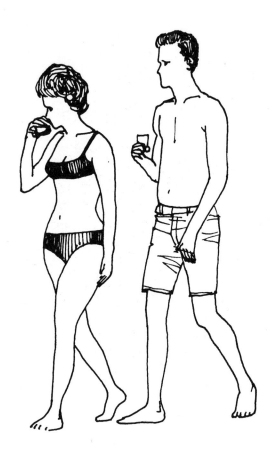

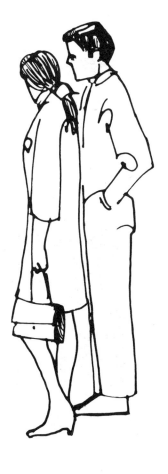

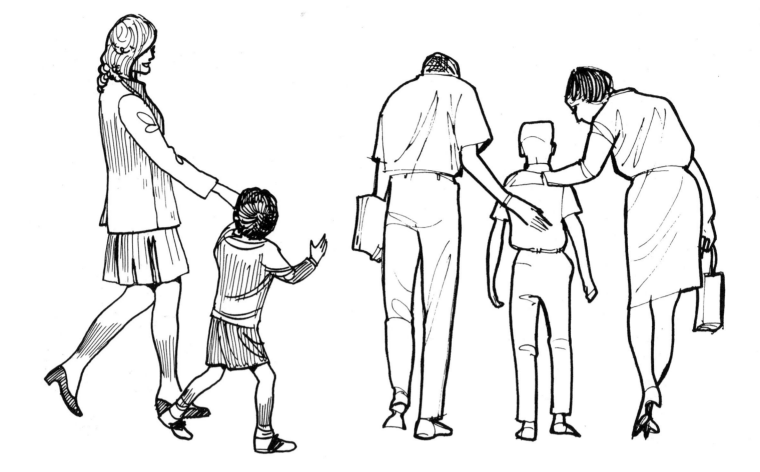

PEOPLE

CHILDREN

SCALE 1/8" = 1'

SCALE 1/4" = 1'

SCALE 3/8" = 1'

SCALE 1/2" = 1'

SCALE 3/4" = 1'

NO SCALE

PEOPLE

MISCELLANEOUS
FIGURE STUDIES

II

TREES

DECIDUOUS

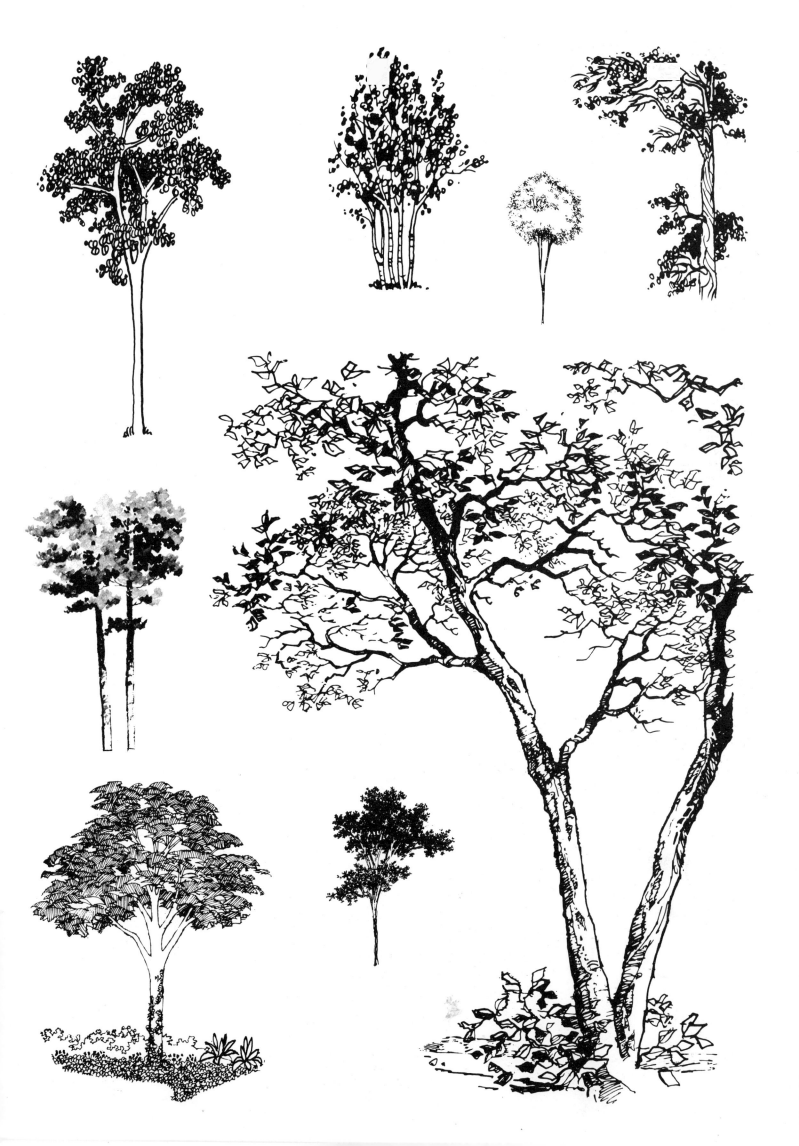

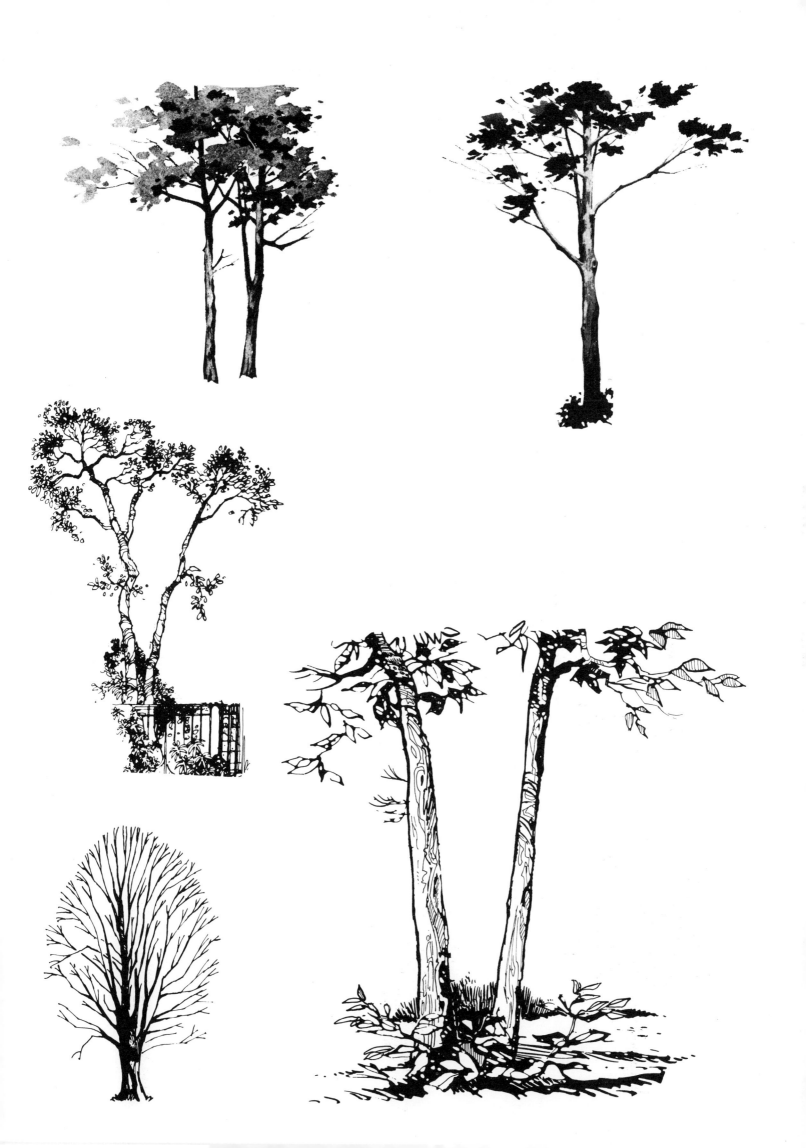

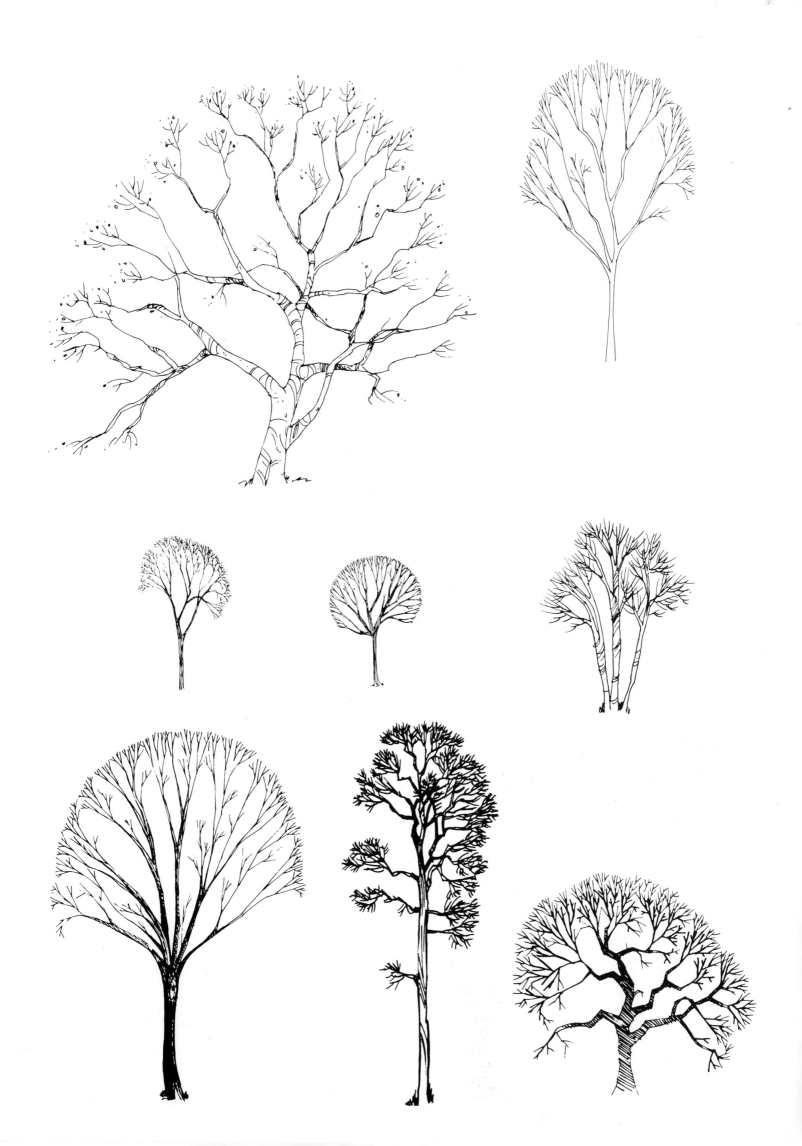

TREES

EVERGREEN

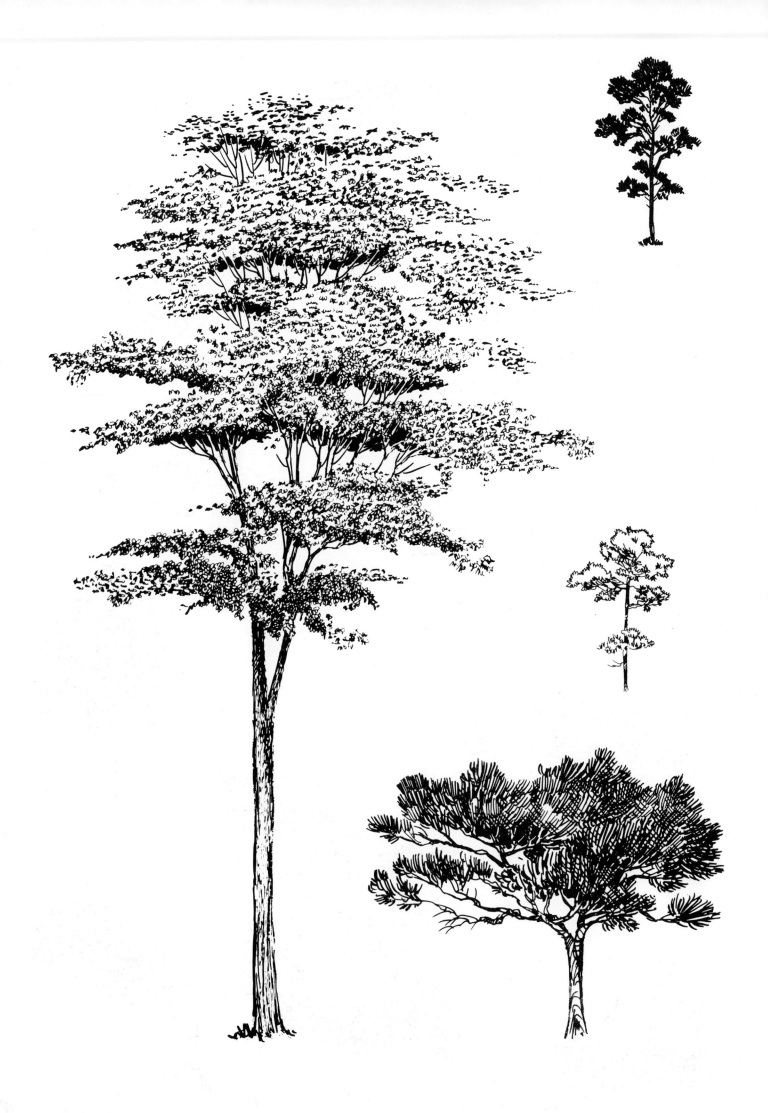

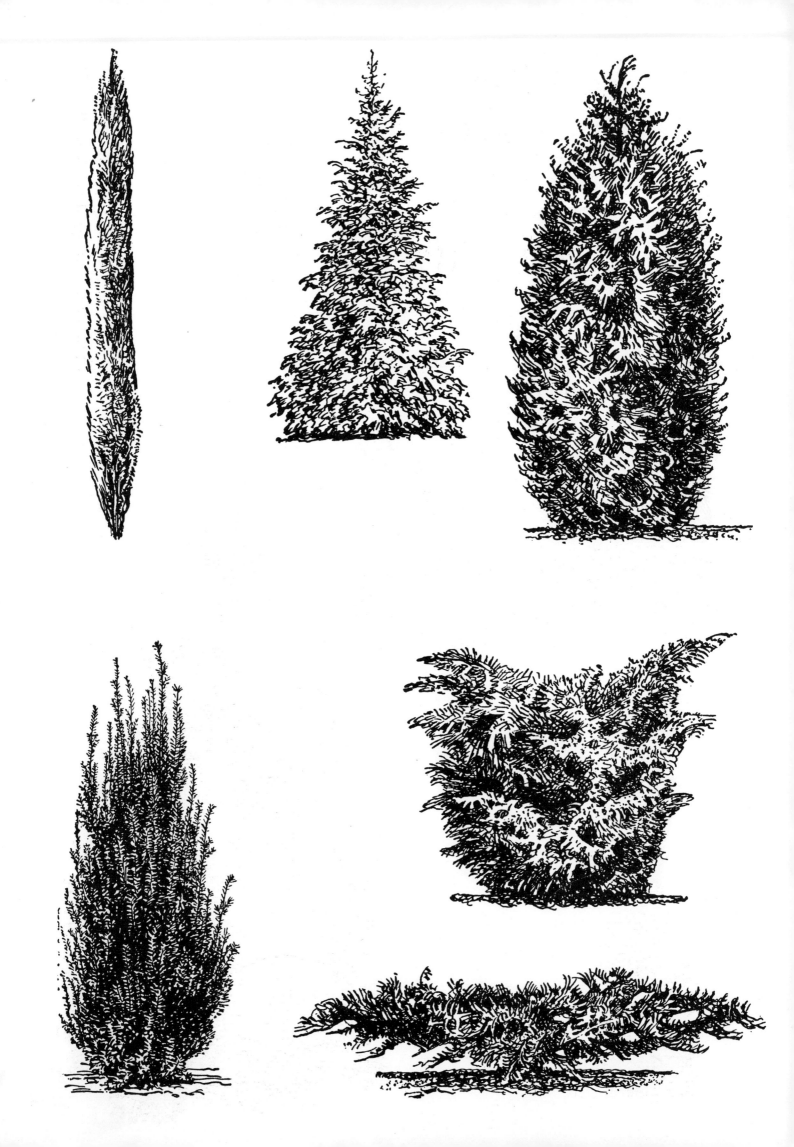

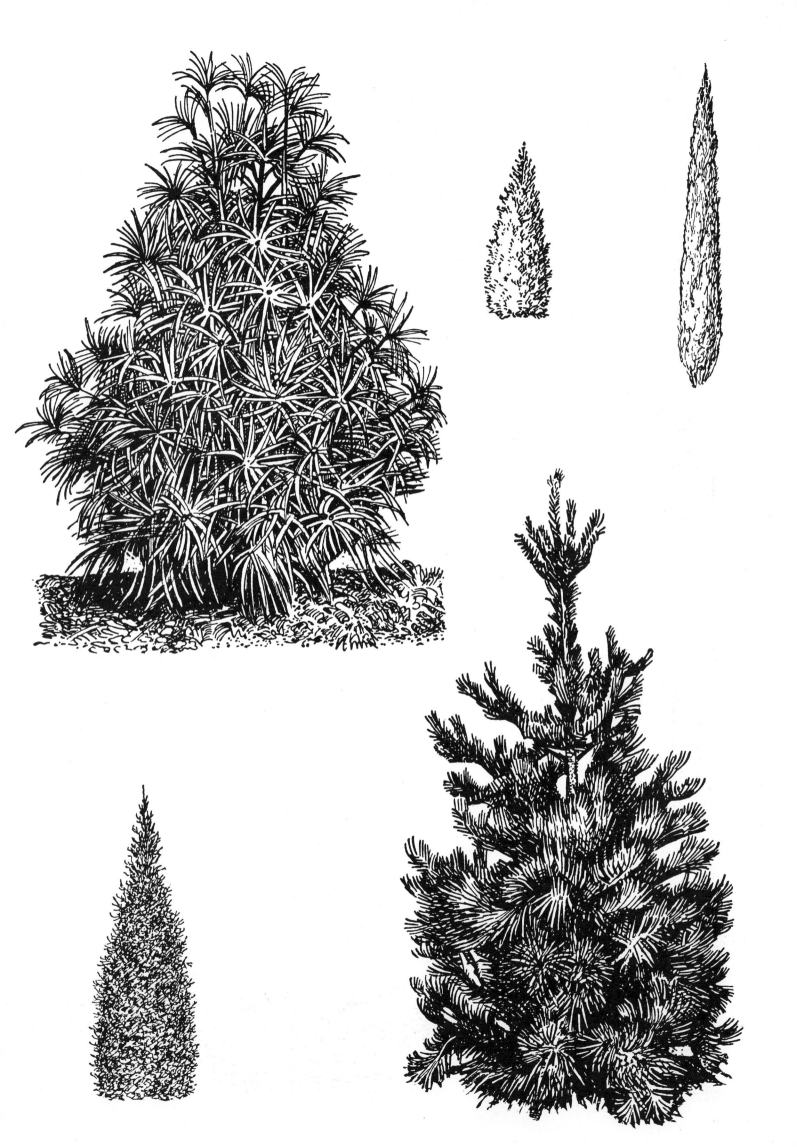

II

TREES

II

TREES

PALMS

II

TREES

PLAN TREES

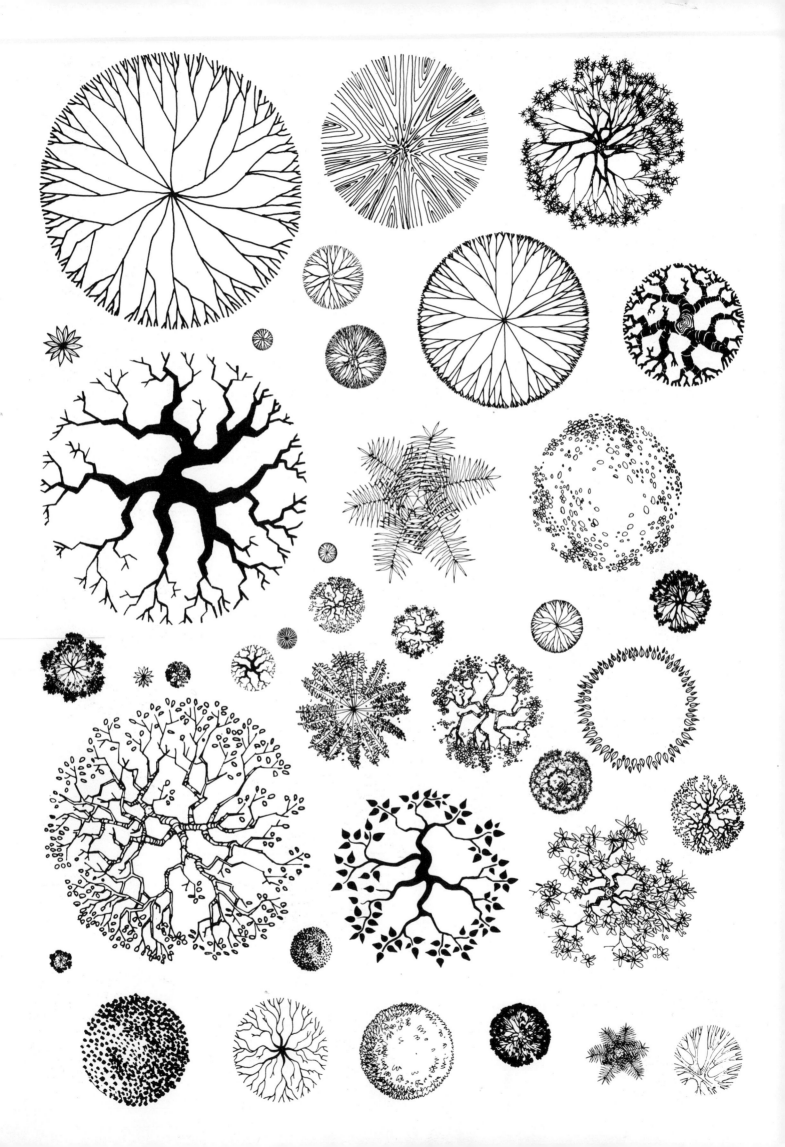

III

PLANTS

PALMS AND FERNS

III

PLANTS

III

PLANTS

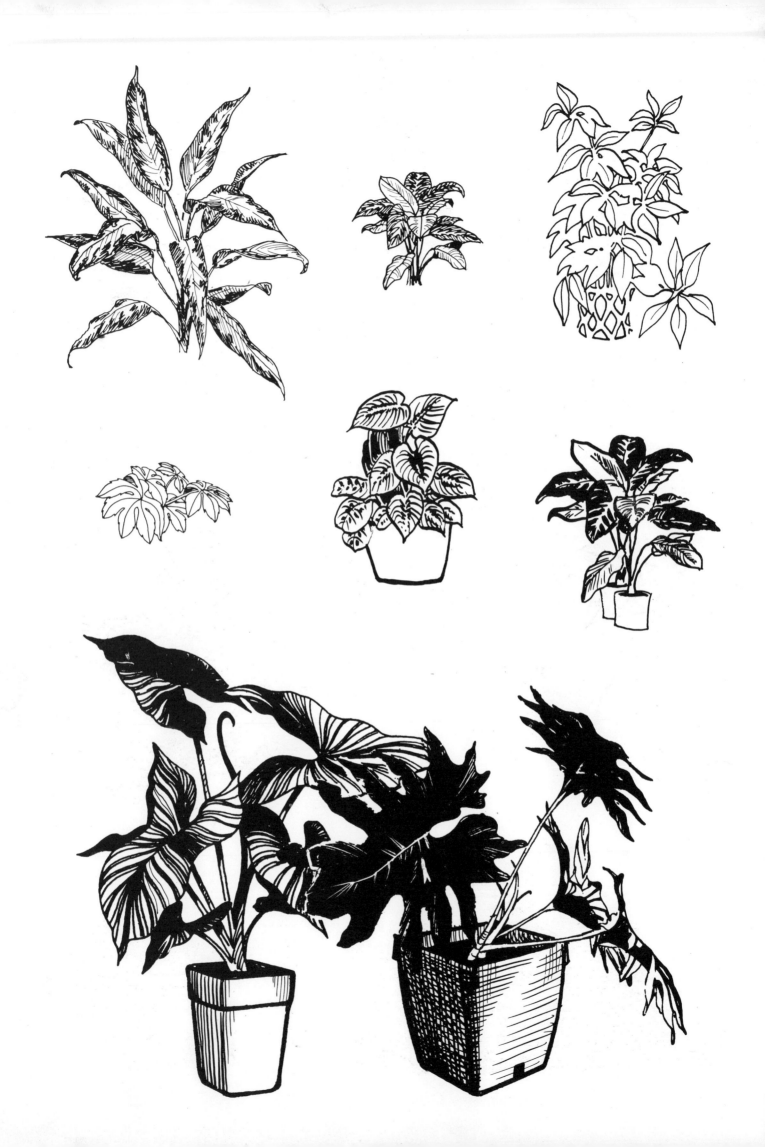

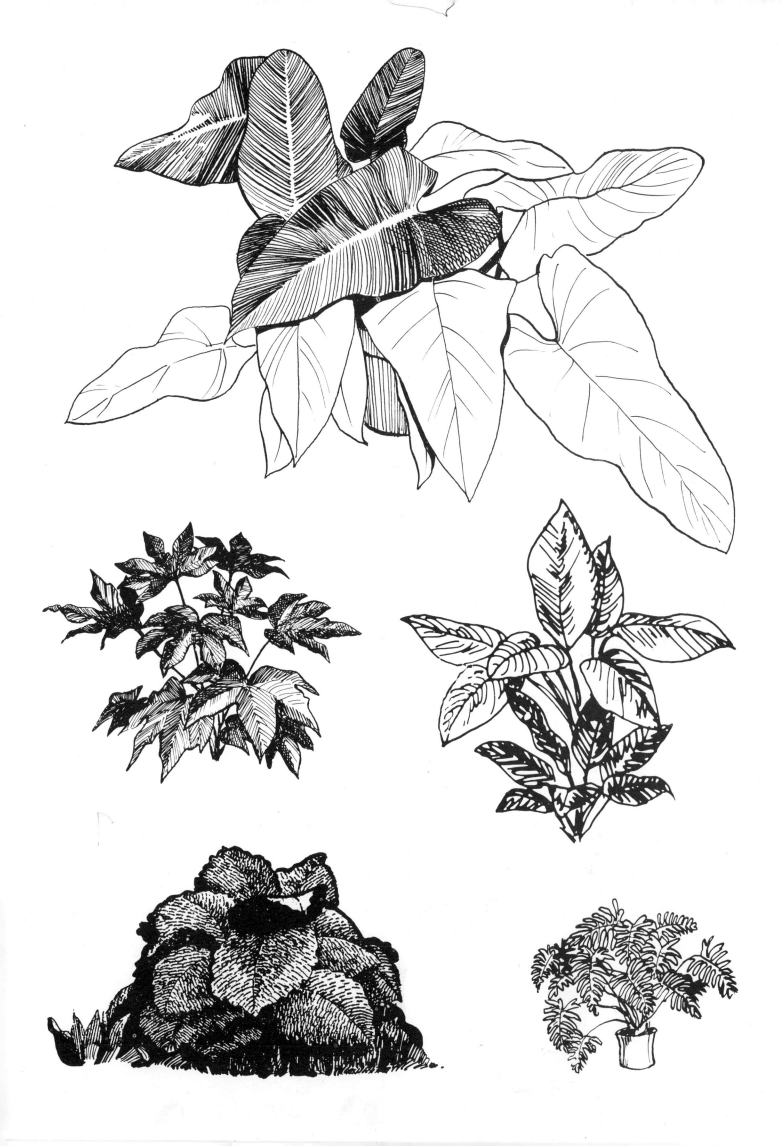

III

PLANTS

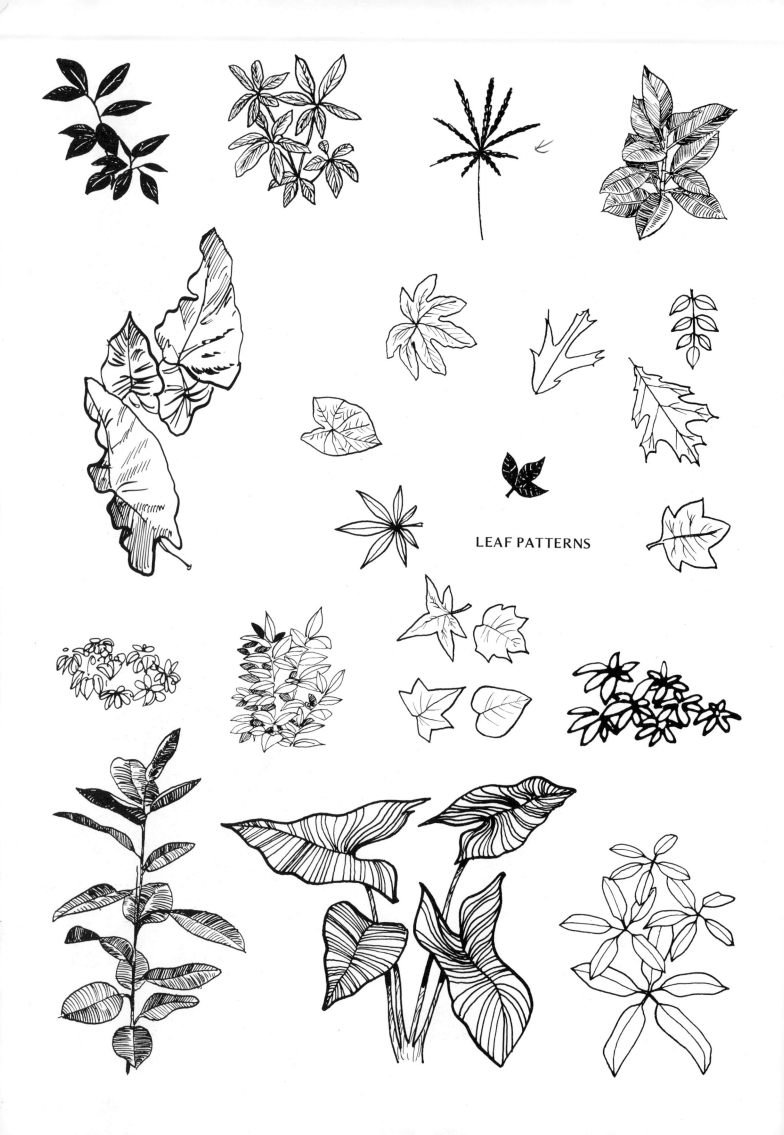

LEAF PATTERNS

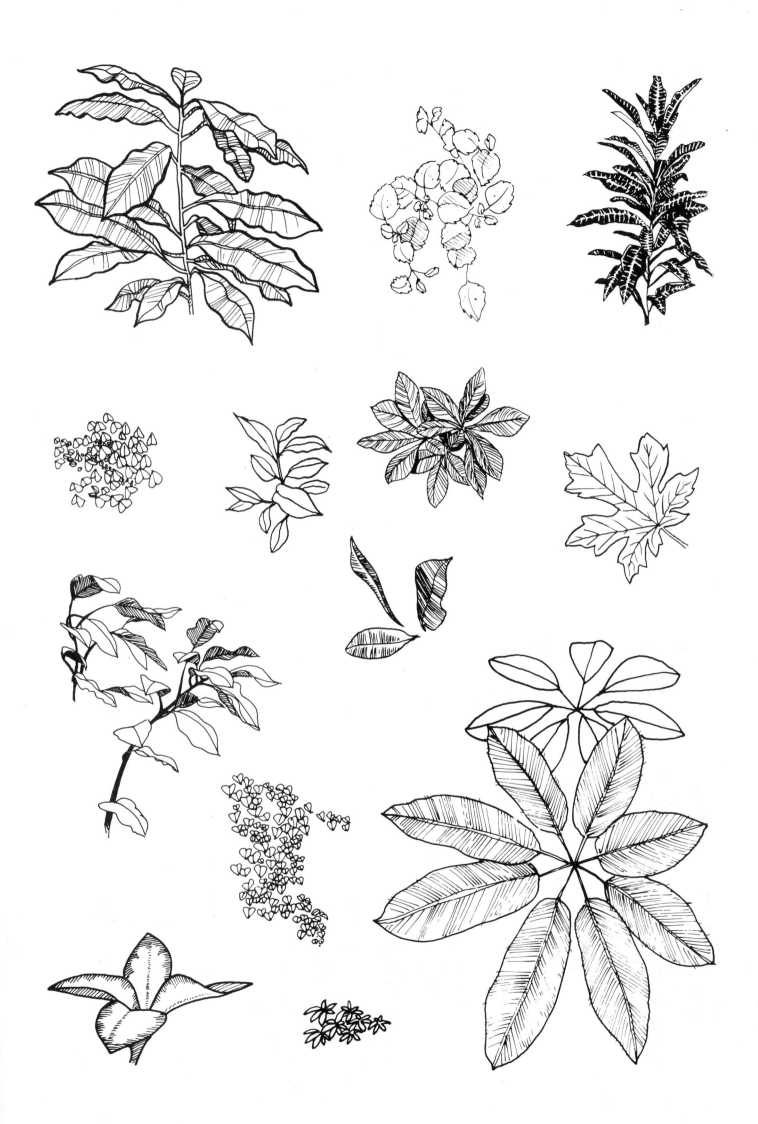

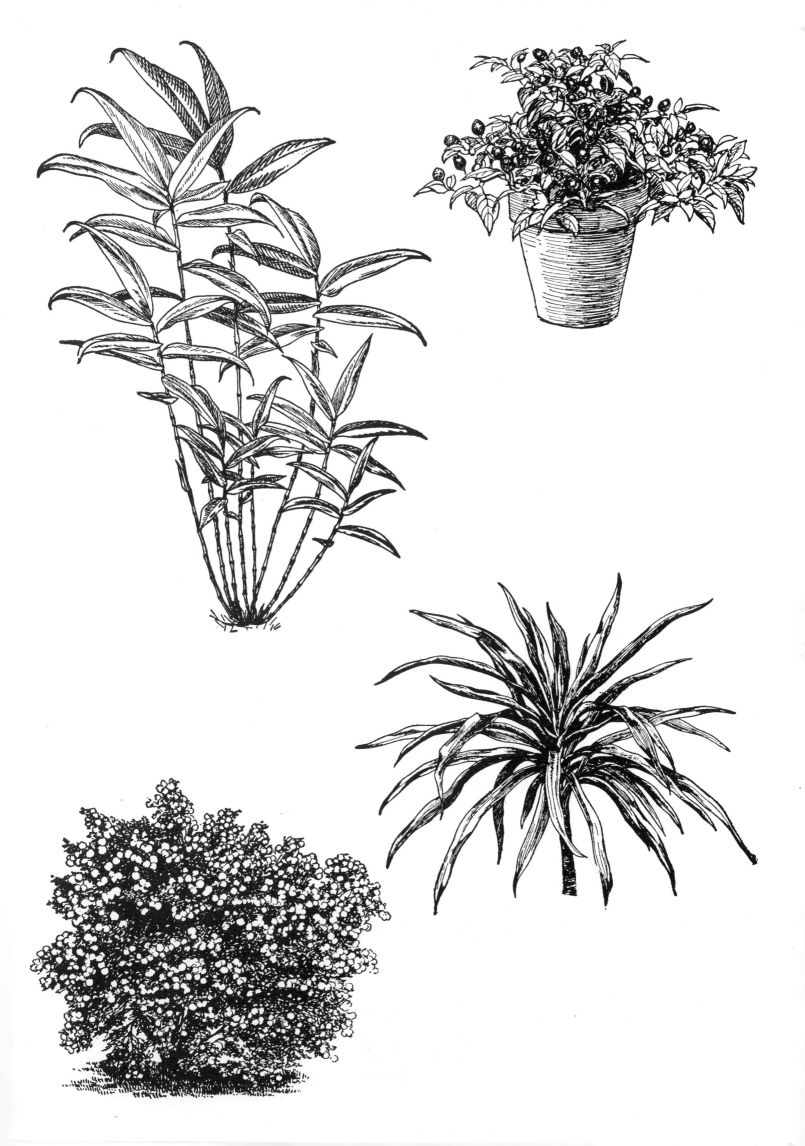

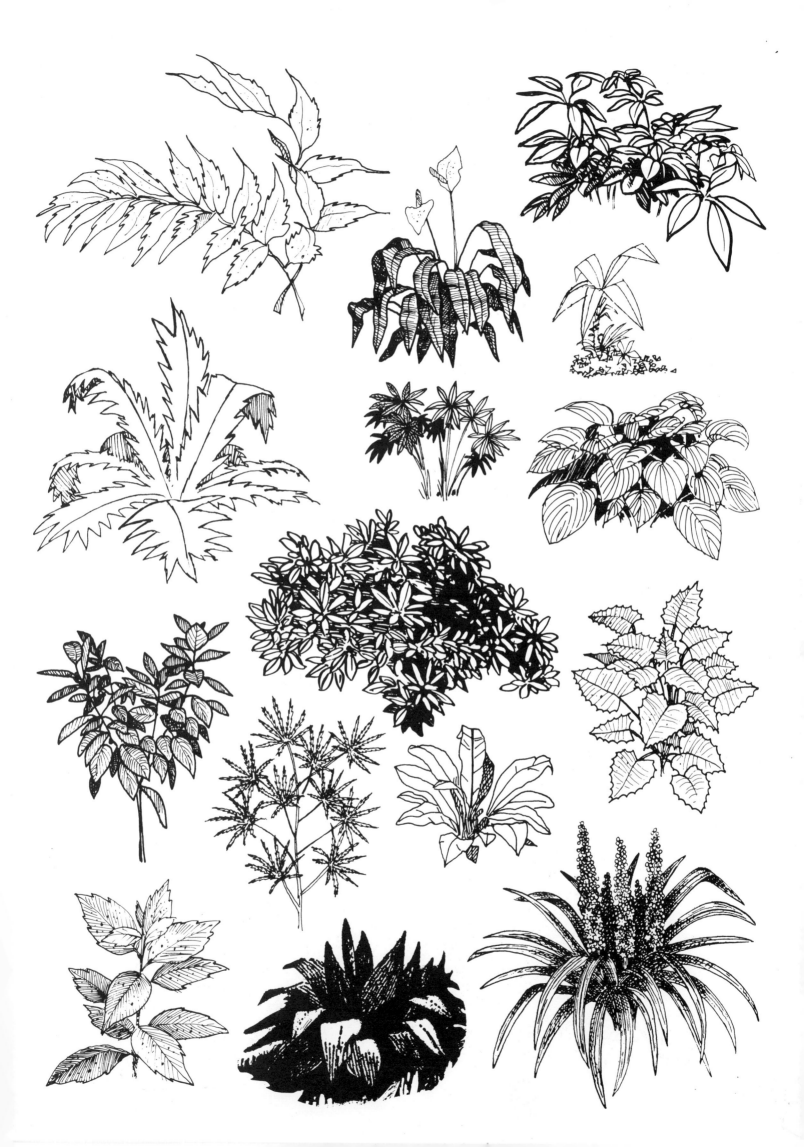

IV

VEHICLES

AUTOMOBILES

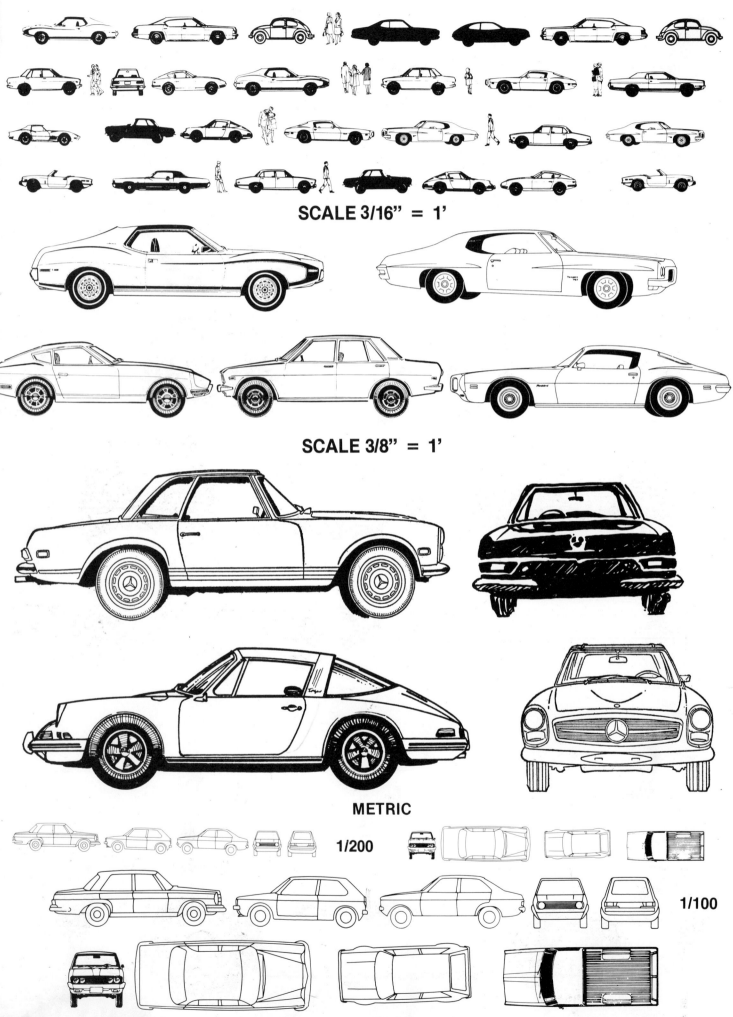

SCALE 1/16" = 1'

SCALE 3/16" = 1'

SCALE 3/8" = 1'

METRIC

1/200

1/100

METRIC 1/50

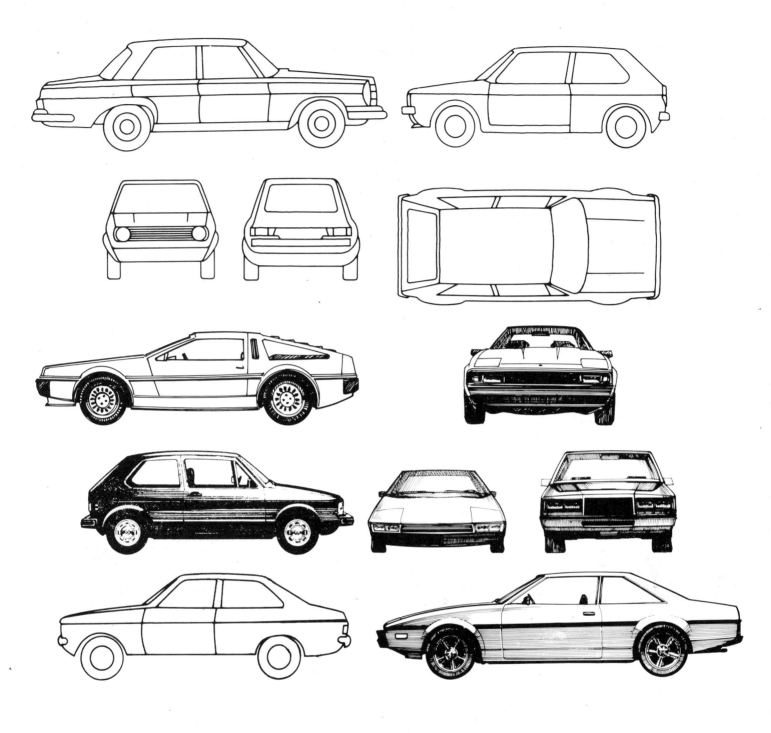

METRIC 1/25

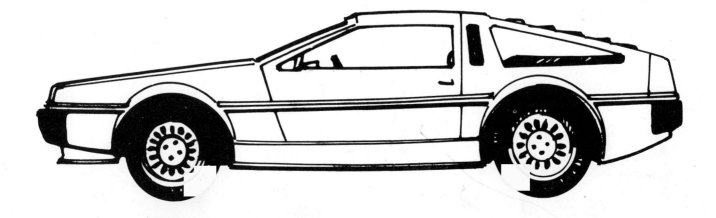

SCALE 1/8" = 1'

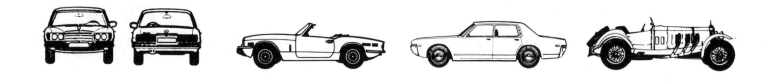

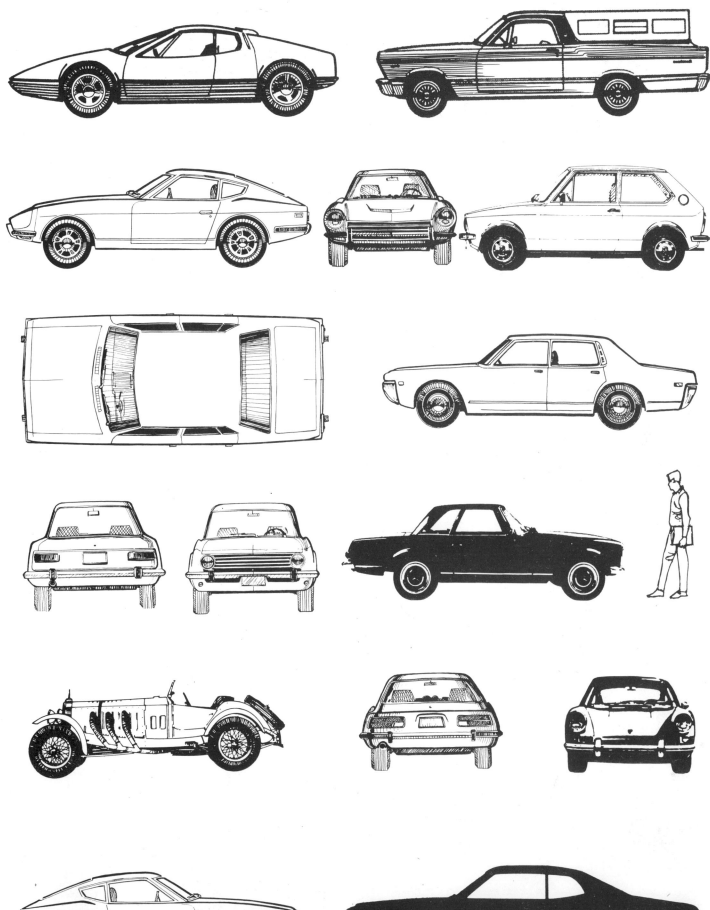

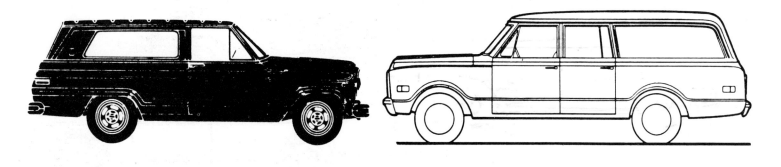

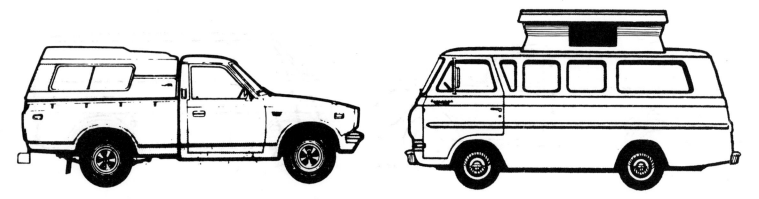

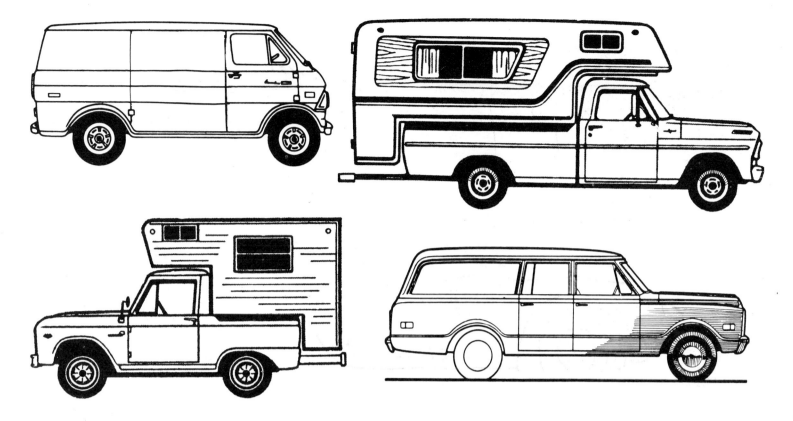

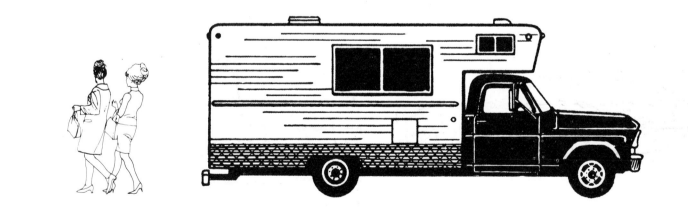

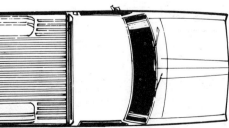

SCALE 1/4" = 1'

SCALE 3/8" = 1'

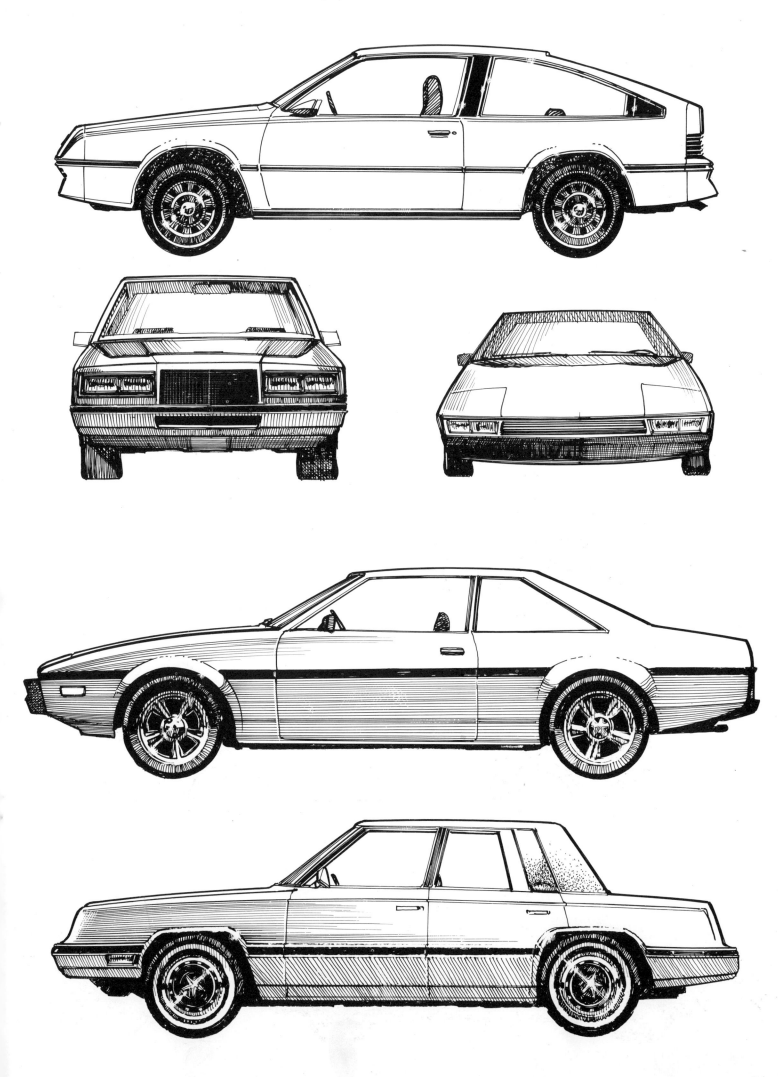

SCALE 3/8" = 1'

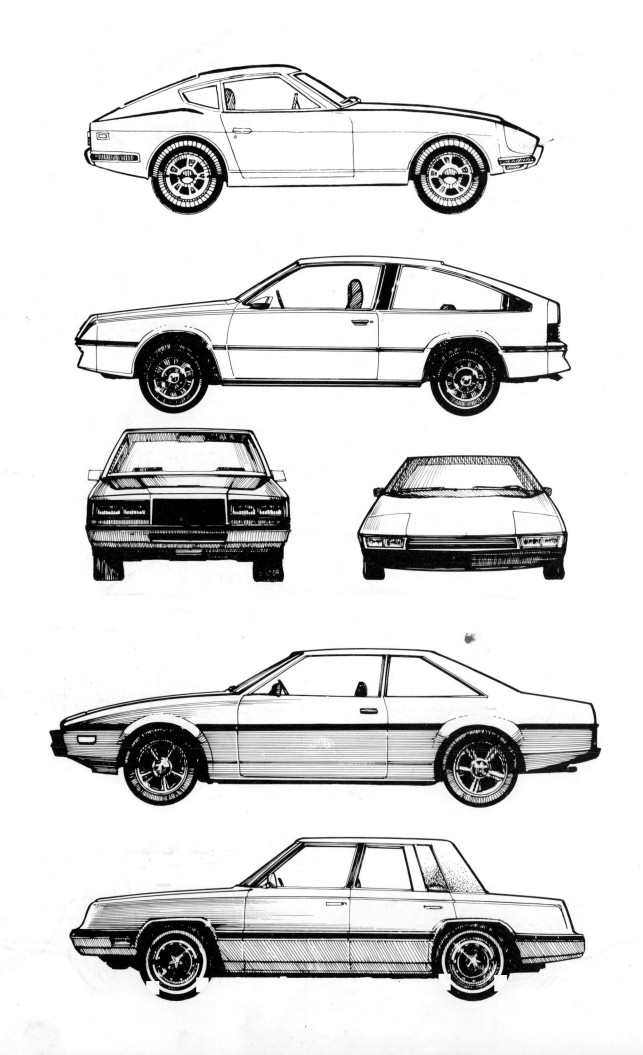

IV

VEHICLES

TRUCKS AND BUSES

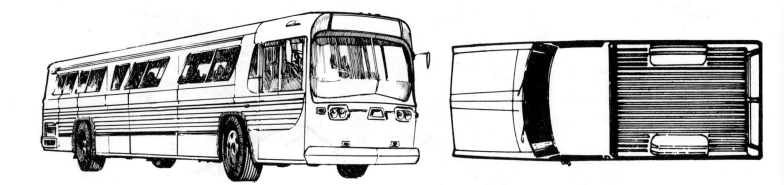

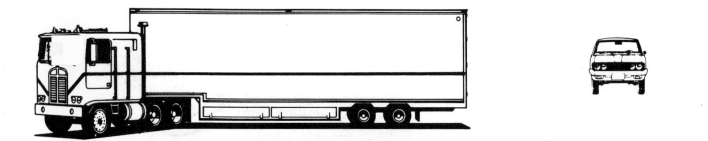

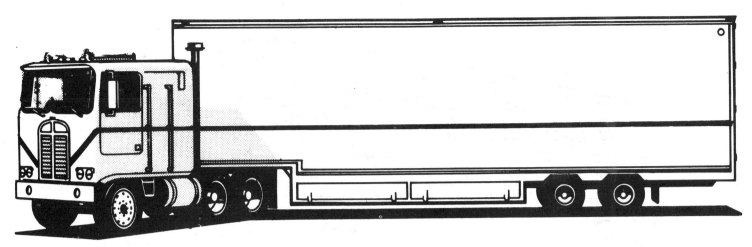

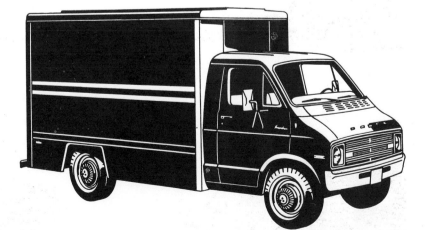

SCALE 1/16" = 1'

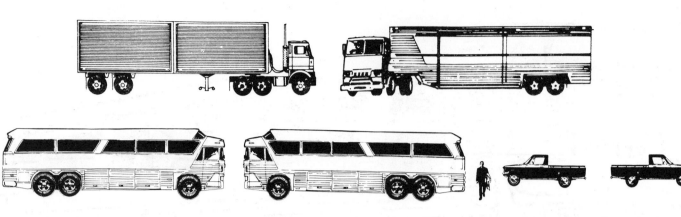

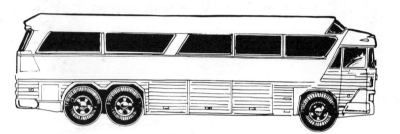

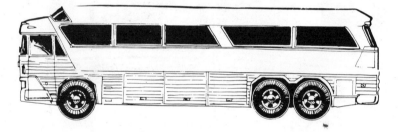

NO SCALE

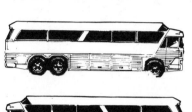

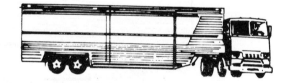

SCALE 1/8" = 1'

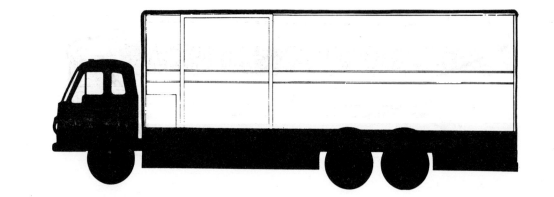

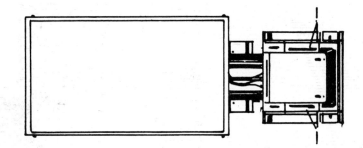

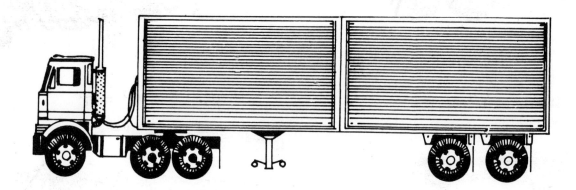

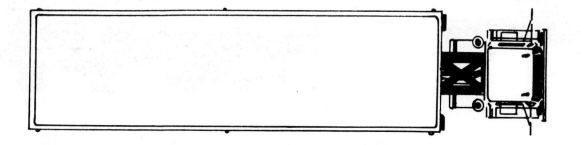

SCALE 1/8" = 1'

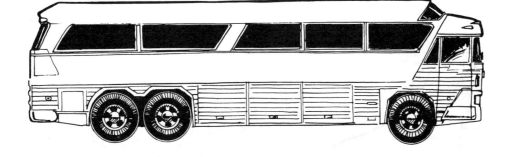

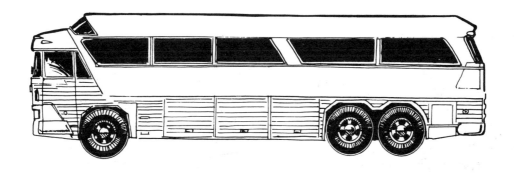

SCALE 3/16" = 1'

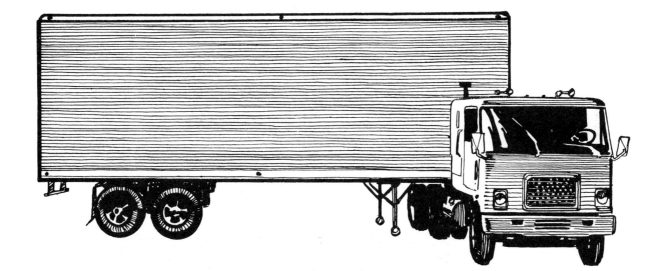

SCALE 1/8" = 1'

SCALE 3/16" = 1'

IV

VEHICLES

BOATS AND PLANES

AIRPLANES   50 SCALE

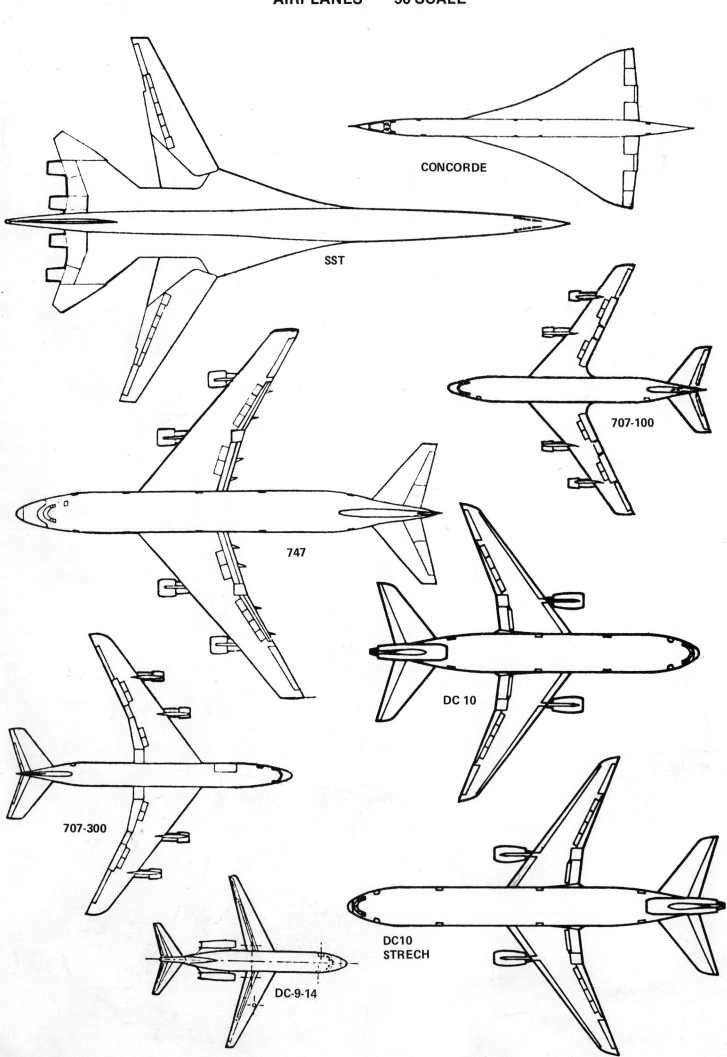

CONCORDE

SST

707-100

747

DC 10

707-300

DC10
STRECH

DC-9-14

727-200

CV 880

DC-9-32

DC8-51

727 STRECH